BUNMI

I Lost Her When I Thought I Found Her

AUTHOR

CLARA MEIERDIERKS

Nee Uwazie

Contributor and Editor
AMINA CHITEMBO

www.claram.net

Editing and Layout by Amina Chitembo.

Cover Designed by Ahsan Chuhadry.

Cover Artwork by Vivian Timothy.

Published by Diverse Cultures Publishing, UK.

Website: www.diverse-cultures.co.uk

Email: publishing@diverse-cultures.co.uk

ISBN: 9798664457001

DEDICATION

To anyone who has experienced the loss of a loved one, I hear you.

To all who are in pain, I feel you.

To all who are in tears, take heart.

For every loss leaves golden memories behind.

"Seashells remind us that every passing life leaves something beautiful behind."

- Unknown.

CONTENTS

(I)

THE AUTHOR

CLARA MEIERDIERKS (NEE UWAZIE) is a multi-award-winning author and much respected active member of the Nigerian diaspora community in Europe. She lives in Germany, her second home with her husband Hagen Meierdierks and daughter Shanaya Meierdierks. She was born in Nnarambia Ahiara, Mbaise, Nigeria, to the late Mrs Elizabeth Adanma Nneoha Uwazie and the late Mr Patrick Uzodinma Uwazie.

Aside from writing and poetry, Clara is a qualified nurse and midwife, quality manager in health (Cert), and holds B.Sc. (Hons) in Health and Social Welfare and an M.Sc. in Psychology. She is a Respiratory Care Practitioner and is currently pursuing a PhD in Public Health, she is researching *the impact on family members of end-of-life patients transiting from curative to palliative care*.

Clara enjoys writing, blogging, and speaking at international events on health and other issues relating to migrants. In her own words, Clara says *"being an author has added much more colour into my life"*.

PREFACE

DEATH IS A SILENT VISITOR THAT plunges a dagger into the hearts of the young and the old alike. It makes one feel sad and helpless wherever it visits. No matter how bitter we think about death, we must at some stage write, paint, sing, and speak about it to let go of our pains and keep the beautiful memories alive.

Bunmi was one of a kind who gave selflessly. She was loyal to all who knew her, alas she succumbed to the holds of death. This death must be compelling and invisible; to steal life at random.

I felt lonely and sad about the death of Bunmi. *"If I could feel this way?"* I silently asked myself, *"what songs would Bunmi's immediate family be singing?"*

Our losses and pains leave us in a fury and wonder about life and death, and what life is all about.

Sing, laugh, get angry, mourn, as you once did…

stay in. We will laugh and drink fruit liqueur and drive away depression. I will sing if you like. Or else let us go and sit in the dark in your study as we used to do, and you will tell me about your depression, and I will put it down in writing.

"You have such suffering eyes. I'll investigate them and cry, and we'll both feel better."
– Anton Chekhov.

Haruki Murakami has been quoted as saying *"Death is not the opposite of life, rather a part of life"*. Anyone can die anytime, and anyone can be a victim, and no one is exempted, and that is why it is 'DEATH'.

Why These Poems?

"No writing is good enough until you, as an author, make a small contribution, the size of a drop, into the ocean of the world's literature."
– Nuruddin Farah.

I wrote these verses of poetry as a way of mourning a friend I lost when I thought I found her. Using powerful emotional language, and play of words, poetic lines, line breaks and repetitions was one significant way of letting out my pent-up emotions, and at the same time keep the beautiful memories of Bunmi alive.

When someone is feeling sad, it is imperative to share feelings with others and not to pretend, in any form. Otherwise, the sorrow could lead to depression and mental break down that could generally be avoided. Depending on what helps you deal with your losses and challenges, do it, for there is no known better way to deal with the pains of death. Every individual is different and deals with grief differently.

Writing this poetry book became one way of not only ensuring that a kind soul is not forgotten quickly, but it is also a way of supporting her beloved family. I chose this style, idea, and subject as a personal way to pay homage to Bunmi, a good and kind friend that went too soon.

In this book, you will encounter painful emotional and touching poems on the topic of the death of a friend, grief. At times; anger towards a careless nation, and words of healing. These words may sound too personal, but that is my way to deal with Bunmi's demise.

In this book, you will also find inspiring, encouraging, and consoling words that could help you in dealing with grief. If you have lost someone, just tap some strength from these poems, for it could help unseal the mind, and heal some silent wounds. None of us knows what happens after the dead are buried, all we do is to cry, mourn and deal with our pains.

How prepared are we, and what happens afterwards? Though death is not visible, it affects everything as is expressed in most of these free-verse poems.

As a multi-lingual author and poet, I think and write in many languages including German, English and my Nigerian languages of Igbo and Yoruba. It is through the lens of these languages that my poems bring the richness of my expressiveness without censorship, and without adhering to specific vocabulary or tonality. I hope you can savour and relish them as much as I have enjoyed writing this book. To help me self-check my words and ensure they make sense to many, I enlisted a contributor to help me polish up the thoughts and readability where necessary. Thus, the contributor to this book is Amina Chitembo. Her job is not to change my meaning and words but to enhance and arrange them in a more vibrant format where needed for your enjoyment.

Personal Reflection Junctions

Throughout this book, you will find strategically placed personal reflection spaces. They are there for you to write your thoughts, your memories, even your dreams. Reflect on what you have read, think about situations where you could have written your thoughts down. Alternatively, simply take time to breathe and enjoy the empty space. If you feel like it, practice, write your own poem. Share it or keep it, that is up to you. The spaces are for you, nonetheless, enjoy it.

Bunmi Korikor

"Those we love and lose are always connected by heartstrings into infinity."
– Terri Guillemets

Born at Iju Ikale local government area; Bunmi attained her secondary school education at Manuwa Memorial Grammar School, Iju Odo. Her family moved over to Okitipupa where they built a house and lived (1977-1981). She worked at Ilaje Esedo local govt. Igbokoda as a typist after her secondary school from 1985 to 1988. She later attended Ondo state school of Nursing, where we first met in 1988 to 1989, she attended

School of Midwifery. From 1989 to 1990, Bunmi worked at Adetade Hospital. In 1991, she moved and was employed by the Hospital Management Board (HMB) in Ondo state as a staff nurse, and later as a head nurse.

Nigeria Haves and Have Nots

Akure is the largest city and capital of Ondo State, South-west of Nigeria. It has a population of 666,000 (Macrotrends, 2020). Its nearest neighbours are Ilare, Idanre, and Ikere-Ekiti. Yoruba is the main tribe in around the intersection of roads from Ondo, Ilesha, Ado-Ekiti, Benin, and Owo. The primary source of trade here said to be agriculture, yam, cassava, palm oil, kernels, okra, and pumpkins. In this region, Palm produce is mostly cultivated for exports. Akure has a university founded in 1981, federal college of Agriculture and School of health technology, School of nursing and others.

Akure is said to be more organised than other states in Nigeria, and remains a favourite place for me, because of the beautiful memories it holds. Laying on the beach, you see big houses and cars, life around Akure is affluent. Nonetheless, it is a stack difference from the reality from other areas which are ravaged by poverty and generally poor quality of life of the people.

Life is not always as good as it should be in Africa. Many places are still plagued by diseases and abject poverty. The Nigerian health care system is poorly developed with no adequate and functional structures (Welcome, 2011)public health not only functions to provide adequate and timely medical care but also track, monitor, and control disease outbreak. The Nigerian health care had suffered several infectious disease outbreaks year after year. Hence, there is need to tackle the problem. This study aims to review the state of the Nigerian health care system and to provide possible recommendations to the worsening state of health care in the country. To give up-to-date recommendations for the Nigerian health care system, this study also aims at reviewing the dynamics of health care in the United States, Britain, and Europe with regards to methods of medical intelligence/surveillance. Materials and Methods : Databases were searched for relevant literatures using the following keywords: Nigerian health care, Nigerian health care system, and Nigerian primary health care system. Additional keywords used in the search were as follows: United States (OR Europe. Even when there are enough health workers, the hospitals are under-equipped.

Gracious God, to whom do we turn?

Poverty looms, people murmur and complain,

But then, no one hears.

What generation with looks of regrets, unshed tears?

With the loudest silence, we watch our glory fall,

Our leaders lead badly,

Ecosystems damaged, air polluted,

As our people get sick,

What a pitiful generation we are,

A generation that plays blind and not bold,

Our people are dying,

Dying at a very young age.

Where One is Born Matters

> *One of the most significant problems of our age is that we are governed by people who care more about feelings than they do about thoughts and ideas.*
> *- Margret Thatcher.*

I wonder if when Thatcher used the above quote, she had African leaders in mind. These are powerful words, and we know they are not mere words because they resonate. Honestly, where one is born matters a lot.

It is not only a lack of food that causes health problems. Where one is born could be a reason of stress which could be a result of our polluted environment. The stress affects our bodies in many ways, such as shooting hormone in the form of cortisone leading to the body responding poorly. Some cases like high blood pressure, kidney diseases, stomach ulcers and even cancer have rooted from stressors, leading to diseases that cause early deaths of our loved ones. We are left to wonder, cry, and shed tears, inform that leave us helpless.

CONTRIBUTOR AND EDITOR

AMINA CHITEMBO IS A multi-award-winning British-Zambian Leadership Development and Inclusion Coach, Educator, Author, Publisher, and International Speaker. She is a University lecturer in Leadership Development, Diversity, and Inclusion. She is a PhD candidate researching on Migrant Women's Self Inclusion into Leadership, and founder of Diverse Cultures businesses. She also holds an MSc in Leadership and Management, and multiple coaching accreditations and certifications.

In addition to co-writing, compiling, and editing many books for others, Amina has authored books on Profitable Teams, Pushing Through Fear, Stereotypes, and Imperfections, and What Serious Executives and Business Owners Need to Know Before Hiring a High Performance Coach.

Amina has been working with Clara (the author as an editor, publisher, and a mentor since they met through African Women in Europe, an organisation that connects migrant women with Europe and beyond. Amina's areas of interest and expertise include Leadership development within organisations and at an individual career level, Migrants women's self-inclusion into leadership positions and helping others to write and publish books.

It is in this capacity that Amina has contributed to this masterpiece.

Contributor's Note and Praise of the Book

"When we give cheerfully and accept gratefully, everyone is blessed."
– Maya Angelou.

Contributing to this compilation of poems by the amazingly talented Clara Meierdierks has been the highest honour anyone could receive. A very special thank you for allowing me to augment to what is already excellent work to make it even more spectacular by reading through, playing around with titles, some verses, acting as the test subject reader. As Mark Shields' quote goes *"There is always strength in numbers. The more individuals or organisations that you can rally to your cause, the better"*. Thus, bringing myself as a contributor in words and Vivian Timothy as the cover are designer to your cause demonstrates the professionalism in your work.

The nature of the subject makes the book authentic and poignant. Yet, the poems within it have a way of captivating the reader's imagination and evoking self-reflection and self-care within all who read it. As someone who has lost many loved ones over the years, I can attest to the danger of unacknowledged grief. The danger of merely trying to get over the loss of loved ones without processing feelings, emotions and dealing with the pain can have serious repercussion.

This book will help anyone who has experienced loss and indeed, those who want to read and relate to the author's style of writing.

Clara has a Shakespearean yet straightforward twist in her writing. The job for me has been to maintain Clara's style and language as best as I can represent her. The nobble acting of raising funds the Bunmi's children is such an honourable act of kindness.

Clara, you are a beautiful person inside and out.

It is a pleasure working with you.

Amina Chilembo

---

1. T'S THE TEARS

We shed tears,
To wash away sorrow,
To fight our hollow,
Nothing strange,
T's the tears.

God's gift to us, Our holy water,
That heal us in sorrow,
Tearing our inners,
Provoking our mental states,
To despair and melancholia,
Wetting faces, and turning the eyes,
To fireworks, tears drop, and drop,
Like the sky bleeding,
T's the sad tears.

Tears are nature's way of letting out,
In grief and loss,
Nature is a way of speaking out,
Of saying goodbyes,
Voicing out pains, anger, frustrations,
T's the sad tears.

Nature's downpour mixed with anger,
Anger that is deeply rooted,

At things beyond us, at death, and ills…
Causing us heartaches,
For places where we are born, are our chain,
Many have suffered extreme pains,
From the loss of someone so dear,
Something so close,
Someone so irreplaceable.
T's sad tears.

People die every day,
And we cry and tears rolls,
And we search our heads, our milieu
For possible consolations.
When we think of the death of a loved one,
An end without return,
We shed tears and feel sad, low and cry,
And let tears drop.
T's sad tears.

The above poem was written to remind us that we all are here by chance, and death has no remedy, and all we do is to shed tears. In this poem, tears are described not only as sadness, but it is also nature's way of healing and smoothening a heavy heart. Tears also can show goodbye.

2.   DECEMBER EIGHTH

I lost my fantastic School of Nursing best friend on December 8, 2018. God knows why... I really thought we were going to meet sometimes soon, but this never happened. Instead, I was told she went too soon, after a brief illness.

> *"The dust returns to the earth as it was, and the spirit returns to God who gave it."*
> *- Ecclesiastes, 12:7.*

I wondered why she left this world, but life has its own laws and controls its laws. We were best of friends in the School of Nursing Akure as we supported one another. Our friendship extended to our families and all around us. She was always around me and never allowed anyone to hurt me. She knew how sensitive I was and did her best for me as a good friend.

Bunmi was from the Yoruba tribe, and I am from the Igbo tribe. The two tribes have historical differences which have trickled to how people work together. In many African countries, tribalism plays a big part in how people get on. It is an old social construct which plays a big part in whether people are treated well as part of an ingroup or not because of their outgroup status. These tribal issues did not apply to us. She made sure I was never treated differently because of my tribe and language. Although I spoke the Yoruba language then but with my Igbo accent which some made jokes of, Bunmi never tolerated anyone making fun of me. That was my dear Bunmi!

William Shakespeare writing about death described death in 'Julius Caesar' as a fearful thing. He stressed in one of his quotes that when beggars die, comments and trumpets are not blown, but the minute any rich man dies, even heavens were described by him as blazing this kind of death. Such is our world.

To me, Bunmi is a star, a kind soul. I shall blaze her departure and let the world know through this book that an Angel has gone to heaven. Yes, like Hamlet's quote *"we know it is common; all that lives must die when the time comes."* After all, Julius Caesar described death, *"a necessary end, that will come when it will."* Yes, it did unexpectedly come, and Bunmi was taking away.

To say all heartaches end with this is far from

reality, for in death thousands of natural shock sets in, for this is a situation that no traveller has ever come back from to tell their ordeals, or what the journey exactly look like. When dead, the deceased turn to ashes and the spirit is gone, with time all is forgotten, all they achieved is gone.

We are all destined to die someday, without return, and we are only remembered by the closest family. Sometimes, even the closest family forgets and carry on with their lives.

We shall not all go at the same time, but we shall go when our time on earth is over. Romans 14:8 reads: "If we live, we should try and live for the Lord; and if we die, we should also try and die for the Lord. So, whether we live or die, we belong to the Lord". Therefore, it is up to everyone to live a good life because, in the end, we will all go, each of us when our time comes.

It is so fascinating to read different ways in which death and dying have been described by writers, artists, and poets. Some have sung it in songs, painted it and even given it names, perhaps, It is these many ways of describing death in the form of metaphor, eulogising and personifying of death that makes it look less callous.

Yes, in our eyes, death is an enemy, a robber, a kidnapper, and a destroyer of joy; still, some people have also described it as one solution to end a protracted illness, painful, incurable cases.

Yes, this same acclaimed death stole Bunmi away from us, to a faraway place where the living cannot reach until when dead.

Bunmi's sudden exit changed a lot in my ways of thinking, as her death brought memories of the loss of my mom, my late sister Stella, Ncheta and many others back. The fact that no one can predict the hour of death chills sometimes. Since we believe in Christ, we will resurrect again after death, this is our consolation. I may not be the only one thinking of you in this form, Bunmi. Still, I am not going to just let your memory slip into the oblivion and be forgotten, that is why my language will continue to flow in your eulogy.

3.   LOSING A SOUL MATE

A close and dear friend,
A friend that I will never see again,
Bunmi Falusi (Nee Korikor),
A friend I longed desperately to meet again,
I searched for her,
Everywhere I could,
Even on Facebook,
No one could tell me where she was.

I wish we did find ourselves,
Remembering the days in Ondo,
In Akure,
Two separate tribes,
One common interest,
Interest to change the narrative of tribalism.

Beauty inside and outside,
Beauty that never hurt anyone,
She gave her best in all,
That which is so treasured,
Her kindness,
Her unconditional love,
Her dedication to friendship,
She gave all.

Bunmi, I wish you were here to say to me. Chi come let us do it this and that way. Together we whispered, as we made our own jokes.

We found soulmates in us,
In Akure,
We learnt the ropes of life,
By untying its knots,
The said that life is a coin,
Which only you can spend alone –
Bunmi you spent your own coin alone,
With no regrets,

Bunmi how I searched for you,
And did not find you,
How I wished I had found you,
I hated how lack of communication kept us apart,
Yes, I thought I found you on December 7
2018,

Alas, you were gone on December 8, 2018,
Dead, lifeless, and gone,
Never to be back again in the physical,
Sad, I lost you to the cold hands of death.

We can never know until we are confronted. We can never know how short life is. Seek your friends, call them, no matter what you are going through. This poem is one way of telling us that tomorrow can be too late.

4. TRIBALISM AND HATE

Tribalism, the mother of hate,
Hate that will not go away,
Murder and killer of progress,
Made and invented by man,
In guise and pretence,
Implanted and deep-rooted,
A blocker and cage of reality.

Now operating as a pest,
In our beloved continent,
Tearing all apart,
And separating friends.

Our handicap in our beloved nation,
A shield that hides crimes,
And blind those who believe in it,
A way backwards,
Our doom.

Enemy of every nation,
A discord in disguise
Destroyer of unity, love, and order,
Misleading and mis-preaching,
The worst enemy of progress,
And the divider of unity.

A pest many abhorred,
A clan we never belonged to,
Though, different in tribes,
We held our values,
The values of unity are not division.

We were different,
With love and understanding,
Respecting one another,
Ready to be the change,
To stop the saga of tribalism,
As we lived in love and with love
To show it is all illusion, our hindrance,
And the narrative that needed an end.

Diversity - not a crime to unity,
And no reason to hate,
In one voice,
We abhorred tribalism,
To show it is possible,
To live together with different tribes.

5. OH! NIGERIA

With one voice, we abhor tribalism.

Nigeria; Africa's most populous country,
Nigeria; has so many ethnic groups,
Nigeria; rich with more than 300 tribes;
They include the tribes of Igbo, Yoruba, Hausa,
Ijaw, Kanuri, Annang, Tiv, Ibibio, Etsako and
Efik, to name a few.
The tribes have different languages and culture,
Nigeria is rich in cultural diversity.

Hausa's are in the North,
Hausas border the southern part of Niger and
West end of Chad Republic.

Igbo tribe; one of the significant tribes
Historically from the Nri Kingdom.
Igbos are Industrious.
Igbos are in South-Eastern.

Yoruba people have a unique culture,
Yoruba language; historically in a centralised
location,
Yoruba people have an Oba as their king.
They are found in the south-west,

Alas! The 1914 amalgamation of Northern and
Southern Protectorate was deemed a failure,
The people are incredibly different
In history, they did not get along,
Tribalism is the order of the day,
Nigeria: your tribalism we abhor,
With one voice, we abhor tribalism.

PERSONAL REFLECTION

Go on, this is your space to reflect. Write something here. Anything!

---

6.   OH, DEATH!

Though, you do not breathe,
But you take the breath away,
Though, you do not speak,
But you make the loudest noise,

Though, you not only strike,
You destroy all,
Though, you do not have senses,
You see, smell all,
And feel only those you want to take,
Though, you are invisible
But visible to those you choose as prey,

Though, you do not have what we have,
But you touch everything when you come,
And set all in chaos and doubts,
Your silent movement makes you invisible,
To steal that which you did not create,
And make them your easy prey,

Oh death, Bunmi did not see you,
But felt your grief,
She wrestled with you,
You took her and made us downcast,

With raindrops that never will dry again,
Oh! Death, Death…

Jeff Goins, a motivational writer in one of his writings, said we need not avoid writing our pains, because of its healing effects.

Yes, in Revelation 21:4 the Bible reads: "He will wipe every tear from their eyes, and death shall be no more, neither shall there be mourning, nor crying, nor pain, any more, for the former things have died, and so is with life." Bunmi is gone, and death shall no more be a topic for her.

7.   WRITING MY THERAPY

I felt weighed down with pains,
And sought answers,
And found none waiting for me,
Looking up in the cloud,
I could hear a notebook and pen,
Whispering and beckoning to me.

They would not speak,
But I heard the messages clearly,
Hastily, I grabbed the notebook and pen to
settle my mind,
Suddenly melancholia, fear, and doubts
melted away,
Words became for me a teacher,
Words; magical, soothing, and healing,
Thoughtfully, I began to unfold my pains,
Writing became my way out.

For a while, I got lost in my world,
Leaving my fears and worries behind,
To make bold the situation in writing,
As I make sense of my emotion,
Through writing,
So many things became clear to me,
My unique self,

My writing, as therapy,
My escape, my courage, and now my healer.

This free poem on writing as a therapy, used play of words in a poetic form, to display the act of letting out emotion on notebooks and keyboards as a way of healing. Some people said they cannot write when in pain, but I have used writing in my darkest situations, and it helped me, and I think anyone should try that.

8.   A SONAK 85B LOSS

SONAK 85b without Bunmi Falusi,
Yes, in School of Nursing we bonded,
And were good friends,
We chatted and laughed together,
We lent hands and extended love where we could,
Bunmi, a darling to everyone,

With smiles challenging to forget,
Our School of Nursing days were not without
challenges,
But her laughter put all at ease,
How we missed those days,
Now you are gone,
SONAK without Bunmi, what an empty feeling.

The joy that you lived a good life,
Remained a treasure for all,
It is an honour for those who knew you,
To remember you always,
And keep you fresh in mind,

Though we were wide apart,
Separated from miles and kilometres away,
After our School of Nursing Akure and Ondo,
Although, I did not get to hear your voice again,

We were never lost,
I will always remember your kindness,
your love and your angelic laughter,

SONAK 85b without You,
But in memory, you remain.
You departed too soon my beautiful friend,
But never completely gone,
Out of those dear hearts that love you,

We cannot reverse or challenge nature,
But it is in my painful joy to keep your memory
On for all to know,
You deserve to be always remembered,
and this I owe you, a good and kind friend you were.
SONAK 85b set will remember you forever.

*"For a sorrow's crown of sorrow is
remembering happier times."
- Alfred Lord Tennyson.*

I wrote this poem with SONAK 85b in mind to
show appreciation to a good friend. Herein this poem
teaches and preaches good team, for the spirit of good
teamwork is the best.

9.   CALLED TO SERVE

We are called to serve humanity!
As we made the most crucial decision of our lives,
We followed the rules,
carried ourselves with respect,
As we choose to dedicate
ourselves to the care of others.
Yes, we loved serving others,
Yes, we worked as a team,
Today after so many years,
Our beautiful memories still linger,

We cared for others,
And made it our passion,
Because we helped them, and they give us
Inspiration,
To work and do good,
T's great to be a nurse.

The joy we derive in serving humanity, yes, we are
nurses. Yes, we were called to serve humanity, we
helped them and they, in turn, help us. I wrote this
poem to honour nurses who choose to serve humanity.
We must praise ourselves, as well as encourage others
because there is dignity in serving humanity.

10. SACRED MEMORIES

We made beautiful memories my friend,
Delightful memories that will not disappear,
Sacred memories that will remain forever,
In me and in that special place in my heart,

We all would have wished to have your laughter
and your gentle soul again, Bunmi,
But now you are gone.
Just as it is written in Hebrews 9;27 that it is
appointed for man to die once, and after that
comes judgement.
Bunmi Falusi as years pass by,
Still, we are left to soak our souls in agony,
As we wonder and keep on wondering, Why?
Why? Why?
Why you slipped away.
Death has done its worst,
Bunmi, nothing can touch you again.

I cannot express or explain why?
Neither in words nor in writings,
Can brighten our rugged looks,
For my readers,
I allow you a sacred space.

To pray for a kind soul,
To let her be in good memory,
With consolations,
Hopes that it is worth living a good life,
Living the first footprint for others to follow.
Yes, in excellent and sacred memories,
You will always remain.

PERSONAL REFLECTION

Go on, this is your space to reflect. Write something here. Anything!

----

11. WHATEVER WORKS

How we let go,
Becomes our excellent task,
How we speak of death,
Becomes our narratives,
That decides how we cope.

Everything today is narrated,
In ways of our society,
To suit them,
Odd to others,
But real to many,
Gentle we will stick in our wisdom
That guides us to act in safety.

There is no known recipe,
Except for individual recipe
Whatever works for you,
Go for it,
Sing, dance, paint, write…
If it helps,
Do your own thing,
Cry your own cry
Change the narrative,

Speak your words,
And let your words,
Be your healer, your courage,
Plan your pains,
And do whatever you suit.

I wrote this poem to encourage the bereaved to mourn their loved ones in ways that are not pathological because there is no legalised standard way of mourning; instead, individuals choose the way of mourning.

12.　　SUDDEN EXIT

Celebrating my only PlayGirl

The sudden exit of a mother,
The sudden exit of a loving mother,
A good mother that went too soon,

To what can I compare the sorrow,
Experienced from the sudden death of a mother,
And a good friend?
The pride and hold of the family are lost with
the sudden exit of a mother.

The mother, the woman, the friend,
Known for her patience, endurance,
Hard work, dedication, and proper management,
She cries when there is no food for the house,
She is familiar with all manner of hardships,
The sudden exit of a mother makes it all harder.

When any member of the house is sick,
Or has a problem she calls herself,
Down in chains of worries,
She gets shattered in thoughts thinking of solutions,
Ready to give up anything for her family,
Much is lost when the mother, the woman of
the house exits suddenly.

Families have been explained to have fallen apart,
Grief-stricken and have suffered bitterly.
And become sick at heart,
When the strong pillar no longer exists,
Kids become confused because mama is not
there again,
All are deserted with empty thoughts,
That is the sudden exit of a mother.

The husband becomes a widow and is helpless
without her,
The whole house weeps night and day,
Refusing to be consoled by anyone,
As no sorrow could be compared to the sorrow
of a sudden exit of a mother.

13.   MOTHER IS SUPREME

Mother is supreme!
She is the pillar of every family
It is easy to understand why,
She provides clear direction,
The mother's role is supreme
in the family and society.

14.   WRITE AND LET IT OUT

I write to encourage others,
To cry and drop emotion in creativity,
When I write, I make it my temple and me?
Write and let it out.

A healing method that soothes,
Consoles and give hope to troubled hearts,
When I am happy, I write,
When I am sad, I make it my companion,
A pillar to lean on.

There is much I could put down in writing,
Some unspoken words,
Phrased to suit the situation,
Things I could not say in words,
I say in writing,
Emotions that are difficult to express,
I create in my words,
I let it out.

15.   IT GOT HOLD OF YOU

Bunmi, death may have laid on you,
Like an untimely frost too heavy for you to push away,
In the end,
It got hold of you,
It slew you with its gross weight.

You must have felt this freezing pain,
A pain that only you could describe,
But cannot tell anyone,
Because death got you.
Oh! The death that has taken your sweet breath,
It made your eyes closed forever
It got hold of you.

I know all must come to dust when nature wills,
For its hold is more robust,
When it comes,
I guess you are sleeping in peace now that you
are gone,
You know no pains again,
It got hold of you.

As nothing again can touch you, not even this
sickness that sent you away so soon,
and caused your journey's end on this earth,
leaving us with hearts full of melancholy floods,
as described by many poets
It got hold of you.

16.   YOUR EXIT

It is heart-breaking when loved
ones go too soon,
Your exit!
Yes, your exit broke our hearts,
Your dying prematurely confused our minds.

Yes, we all struggle with this kind of thoughts,
The battle inside and outside us,
In search of Why!
Yes! Mortality's hands have its grips
permanently on you.

You are still in your eternal home till today,
It shows how helpless humans
are in the face of death,
When I think of you,
All I do is to reflect on life,
And what it means.

Yes, I will continue to tell myself about a friend
who went too soon,
A friend I never get to meet again,
A friend I failed bid farewell,
A friend I will always remember as tears roll down.

You said we were going to meet again,
You told many to look for me,
You promised we will not part,
Now you are gone too soon,
Leaving all with broken hearts,
inner pains, and sleepless nights
Your exit.

17. YOU ARE OUT THERE

Sometimes I walk out alone,
Hoping I could meet you
somewhere, Anywhere,
I know you are somewhere out there,
Physically not present,
But in memory treasured and is ever-present,
I know thoughts cannot bring you back again,
But forever you are treasured
You are out there.

It is fine to feel and think of you,
Never will we let you slip away,
Since you are gone too soon,
We cherish every moment
we spent together in Akure,
These were beautiful moments,
Moments we never get to repeat,
Such is life,
We will forever miss you,
You are out there.

Everything about you,
Your kind ways,
Thank you, Bunmi for the time we had together,
I remembered your birthday,

It must be such a sad day for your children,
your husband and most of us,
Yes, you were supposed a year older,
But you left, you went too soon
You are out there.

Every passing day,
Reminds me a lot about you,
and brings a kind of hope,
Hope that you would be back
from your journey someday,
You are out there.

Yes! Days still seem fresh,
Like its yesterday,
You left too soon,
Soon, soon, and just too soon.
You are out there.

No matter how we feel about our loses, once we pick
up to write, we discover we have a lot to let out. Above
all, the above poems represent how I dealt with the
loss though writing and hope.

18.   BUNMI WHERE ARE YOU?

Everyone needs you,
Come back because your husband feels lost,
And your children do not know who to talk to

What is worrying about them?
The world looks unfriendly,
and things are looking worse,
But you are gone, gone too soon,
It is not the same again without you.

Bunmi where are you?
It looks dull without you,
Without your smiles,
I hope always to see you,
I am still searching for you,
Hoping you will come back again,
I am shouting inside me,
In a noisy and loud world,
But you are not hearing,

Perhaps you will hear your children
and husband?
They cry because of you every day,
Blessing, Layo and Ope keep
waiting for their mom, with the same question,
Everyone that knows you are asking,
Bunmi where are you?
We miss everything about you,
Your gentle way of doing things,
We miss it.

Your beautiful way of calling our names
Still rings my ears,

Oh! Bunmi where are you?
You gave and never wanted anything in return,
You were good inside out,
That we have always known,
Now you are gone,
Bunmi where are you?

Bunmi time goes by,
We heard of your demise.
We did not only cry so loud,
but we also went so low,
You sparkled, and you were cheerful on earth,
So, you will continue your cheerfulness in heaven,
It took a while to realise you were gone.
Bunmi where are you?

19.   I WAS NOT THERE

I was not there,
I could not understand,
I heard, and that broke my heart,
Bunmi I could not even get to speak with you
I was not there.

Not to talk of meeting you again,
To hold your hands,
To whisper and share our jokes,
To hear you call me Chi-Chi,
And I will laugh at that,
I was not there.

I imagined the tumult,
The sorrows that clouded the air,
On this fateful day,
Everything changed for me,
I will never be the same again,
Without your beaming and flashing smiles,
Without a beautiful mummy,
I was not there, my good friend.

This poem is straight from the heart. I miss my friend
Bunmi, and I kept on wondering where she has gone.

Why now? The question continues. When anyone close dies, all we do is, hope upon hopes each passing day that they just went somewhere and would be back again someday.

20.   BUNMI - A GOOD FRIEND

"For death ends a life,
but it does not end the friendship."
- Robert Woodruff Anderson-

I met you a humbled and loving person Bunmi,
You made me believe in nothing less,
But in good friendship,
You came into my life and left a print,
Something suitable for which I am grateful.

You spoke kind words,
And crack jokes that put all at hysterics,
You were indeed a good friend,
Irreplaceable,
It is hard to believe you are gone.

Friends are so rare,
Best friends never cease to be,
even when wide apart,
We were wide apart,
But the thoughts of that past,
Never ceased.

You made me laugh and feel good,
What a good friend I had in you,
And the hopes of meeting you again someday
become a real desire,
You were ever ready to listen to others,
We did a million little things that kept our
friendship fresh in mind, even when apart,
Those beautiful things we shared together,
Post to post never forgotten,
Those whisperings and jokes,

Bunmi, meeting you meant a
lot and still means a lot to me,
Even more, now that you are gone,
But I take solace in God,
And herald your person.

All those years we were separated,
I prayed with the sincerest hope,
To see you again,
And now, you are gone,
I thank you for all that you left in my life,
A print for which I am forever thankful.

When I look back,
I do it with ease of thoughts,
About   all the things we did together,
Both good and bad moments,
Full of Love, a good friend,

We cried together,
Laughed together,
Did a lot together,
We had time to listen to each other,
My good friend,
Lucky that we had beautiful times as friends,
We talked to each other with ease,
We never asked too many questions,
Nor doubted each other,
We trusted each other blindly,

It was a good friendship,
And I valued it a lot, even when you are
Physically gone, leaving all in a dilemma,
You remain my good friend.

I wrote this poem to thank Bunmi for being such a good friend, for good friends are very rare to come by. This very poem is about real friends. My friendship to Bunmi which saw no-fault, and with this his rare to forget a genuine friend. Such was the kind of friendship we shared.

PERSONAL REFLECTION

Go on, this is your space to reflect. Write something here. Anything!

_____
_____
_____
_____
_____
_____
_____
_____
_____
_____
_____
_____
_____
_____
_____
_____
_____
_____
_____

----

21.   DILEMMA OF DEATH

False faces hide terrible losses,
To which only the heart knows,
As we clamour to grief,

We Search the eerie head and hearts,
That now a home for worries,
Confused thoughts mingled with misery,
Nights of sleep lost to death,

Thoughts confused and crowded,
Head pounding from worries,
With full eyes staring up,
And not seeing anything,

Oh! Power of thinking lost,
As seated hearts race,
With horrible images run through the minds,
Things are once seen as usual before,
now, abnormal.

One's own head pounds,
The heart races over again,
Inside, I explode with various thoughts,
The thoughts that were struggling within.

What is best, the head asks,
To scream, cry and explode in thoughts,
Mind in the dilemma that would not let go,
O Merciful powers give back thoughts,

One would go through a lonely path,
With atmosphere filled with silence,
To confront this dilemma,
Sadness is the loudest in time of death.

Here I walked this path, in silence,
Thoughts hung heavy all over me,
Weighing me down,
With misery,
That never truly will leave,
A gaze that never truly will see beyond
dilemma,

And pleasures that will remain unusual,
With thoughts inside shut up in the head,
With sleepy eyes half dozing,
And minds refusing to settle,
All captured in a dilemma,

Oh God, I cried,
It is confusing,
I wrap myself and search for a way out
out of this dilemma.

This poem is about the dilemma that all in grief have had to suffer. We get tormented with horrible thoughts of blames on what we did and what we did not do for our loved ones, never mind, grieve, but never grieve yourself to pathology, stand on God's ways. I suffered it and thought this should help many struggling with pains of grief to talk about the confusion, commotion we all go through when a loved one dies. Such is my way of encouraging the bereaved. For death brings with its dilemma.

22.   NO ONE CARES!

What is wrong,
I remembered the years back as a child,
When people lived in old age,
People were happy,
And life was fun,
NO ONE CARES!

Sad times are now,
Careless times everywhere,
Bad people, corrupt leaders,
Neighbours hate,
Leaders insensitive,
All hopes dashed!
Even when they forbid me to interpret,
I report this
NO ONE CARES!

For memories are sent to Golgotha,
And people are weary and cry for help
Many understood me,
And many with insane root,
That imprisons their reason.
They watch breath melt into the air
The land is left to dry,
Litter everywhere.
NO ONE CARES!

Wealth in the hands of few,
For the rest habitation is uncomfortable,
Germs move freely,
And yet no one cares,
People get sick,
No one cares,
Young dies, and old suffer,
Still, no one cares,
The earth turns hostile
Horrible imaginings.
NO ONE CARES!

23.   WHO CARES?

My thought, who cares?
Many are suffering,
We are helpless,
We hear nothing,
But suppressed voices.
For groans are not heard,
Who cares?

For the sick have no place,
Clinics with doctors and no equipment,
Chance will help some,
We maimed the earth.
Nature is exploited, plundered, devoured
By the vultures bred by Man,
through bad leadership,
But who cares?
Bad policies, racism, tribalism, Religious
fanatism, terror, war, ecological destruction, man
Slaughter, premature deaths plague us,
People have come to enjoy the silence.
People accept that everything is God's will.
All ills, if untimely, are not God's will,
But human ills
Who cares?

Born out of wickedness and greed,
Resulting in negligence of our environment,
Causing sickness and suffering,
That is leading everyone to misery,
Breaking hearts while leaving holes
With no physicians in view,
Who cares?
We must care!

24.　　　IS THAT ALL?

We are losing control,
Control of self,
Control to do good,
We are choosing the wrong path,
We make the wrong the norm.

Is that all we worked so hard for?
We struggled together and now this,
We are losing our loved ones so early,
Early and they are going too soon.
And we are remaining broken,
Broken with our eyes sunken from
tears caused by our losses.

Let us speak and write our heart free
Each in her way,
Enough, premature deaths,

We would want to call them for justice,
But we cannot do much, in a society
vast and corrupt,
In a society made up of different and differences,
In a society widening apart,

From its divide and rule,
No, no check, no balance
No repentance,

A nation losing its wards,
With no meaningful action,
A Collapsed nation pretending to be breathing,
Sinking in the ocean of corruption,

Pretending, so far from people,
Shutting doors to complaints,
Stopping cries outside,
Telling us, all is well...
Is that factually true?
Is that all?

The above three poems are an attempt to make sense of what is going on in our country and how we have all collectively failed nature. Incidentally, most of the sicknesses could have been controlled. Instead, our loved ones are dying prematurely, out of carelessness, and who cares?

25.   EVERYONE GETS HURT

When I heard of Bunmi's death,
I was hurt, and I cried,
I cried for my people, for my loved people,
For my nation,
They are leaving us sick,
Loathing and masking,
Pretending and saying they will not hurt us,
They are hurting us,
Everyone is hurting us,
And anyone can get hurt.

Wish I could tell them this,
Tell them exactly what they are doing,
How they are failing us,
Closing eyes to reality,
And making our lives a misery,
Thinking it is nothing,
But this is something,
Something they shut out,
Out of their minds.

Making us believe it is their best
That they offered,
But they are hurting us,
And pretending not to know,

They are hurting us,
Everyone is hurt,
And Everyone will get hurt

I wrote this free verse to poetically warn aspiring leaders, to do the right thing, otherwise, everyone gets hurt, and everyone will get hurt in the end. When leaders decide to loath, and rob the masses, they not only deprive, they hurt us all. And in the end, all that lived will die, when the time comes, so why not do the right thing.

26.   OUR CAREFREE WORLD

A friend who gave,
But slumped at the carefree world,
They came and preached illusion,
Deceiving and pretending,
That they were friends,
They are not friends,
They are our illusion,
Our impostors
And now our pretending masters.

The conquered and made it their world,
Washed our brain,
Told us their good, lousy stuff,
Alas! We did not only believe them,
We abandoned our mother nature,
To follow their rules and lived their world.

A carefree world that has brought us misery,
Sickness, diseases, and premature deaths,
Nature is replaced with technology,
As their thoughts became slogans,
"White is good, "Black is evil",
Ecosystem, Climate became a thing of technology
And a topic for the Western world.

And lo! All were excited at the 'Messiah'.
Yes, we all jubilation as we embraced all.
Replaced all, even when we do not
seem to understand it all.

The masters stood, conquered, and exchanged
Our nature, to create a carefree world,
Where they all come to the stage to display and act
A carefree world where only the most reliable fit.

They stay to rule upon us,
Make rules that suit them,
Natural foods now replaced with
chemicals and preservatives,
Yes, another source of ill-health.

Drugs kill instead of a cure,
T's is our carefree world today,
A place not for less privileged,
Our carefree world...
Bad news for many of us.

This is the only way to express what I think of our world today. Our world today is crazy. I struggle with how we are cutting our lives, causing death by our errors, and destructions. God did not create death. He gave us everything.

27.   BAD NEWS OR TORTURE

Yes, lousy news carries feelings,
That pounds and sets the heart racing,
And the lungs struggling for air,
It gives a kind of feeling that irritates the tear
gland and because rainfall from the eyes,

It makes you gloom, sets the mind ponder and
struggle for answers,
Answers that will never come,
Answers that make us lose balance
and sanity.

Yes, this comes up when a close person dies,
When we lose something dear,
When did we wish we were there?
When did we wish we could have had answers?
Solutions, and have the best doctors, surgeons
to heal a loved one.

All wishful thoughts take over,
As we hope for all the magic and miracles,
To raise our dead loved ones,
How we ever wished it never happened,
It never comes in bad news,
Oh! Hearts are pierced with thorns.

Misery becomes a long-time companion,
Destroying hopes and plans,
Throwing one into doubts,
Searching as to why!
Suddenly plans fade,
All become meaningless,
Turning our joy to misery,
Making us empty and void,
Making us strange in a familiar state,

We cry, scream but no answers,
We investigate heaven,
But help seems far away,
Undo this we cry,
Inside and outside,
Even Prayers are recited and not prayed,
Prayers cease to make meaning,
And we find ourselves far,
far away from self-healing,
Lessons of psychology elude us,

We hope upon hopes,
And we cry,
We complain,
it is okay,
Breakdown,
Go your process,
It is okay,
Dream, your dream,

Doubt, your doubts,
It is okay,
Yes, this is real.

Go through your process,
Imposed no force,
Do it your way,
Do what makes you cope,
Do what you love, and love what you do,
Pray, sing, dance, paint, and write your healings,
And give bad news no time to destroy.

This poem describes how torturing lousy news can be to the body. It is healing and will help you in dealing with bad news.

28.   A MEMORIAL POEM

A memorial poem for a loved one
December 21, 2018
Bunmi's burial,
Being far away from home,
I mailed my funeral oration to her,
Daughter Blessing,
A free poem I titled,
Lost when I thought I found her.

Bunmi words are not enough to eulogise You,
A good friend Bunmi…
We are crying that you are gone,
I tried to close my eyes,
To see you again,
All I could imagine is all that you left,
Our good old days.

Today, we all are bidding you goodbye,
A loving soul, I know if you were there,
You would say to all at your funeral,
Rejoice, go, and wash, eat and merry,
For you have conquered and overcome.

It is hard putting this in writing,
I would just sit and cry,

thinking of all we shared together,
All two girlfriends in the School of nursing
school Akure could share,
No secrets, just our inner world.

Bunmi, I never heard you were sick,
I only heard of your demise,
I did not get to give you encouraging words,
Never knew what pain you passed through,
Maybe there were some important things you,
Wanted to say to me, which you never could.

All I was told was that you asked all to search for me,
Yes, they looked and found me, but you were
gone before I found you, what a tragedy!
I have wondered in my quiet moments,
Why you did not even write
something down for me,
Why you could not make those
journals and leave for me.

You took your hat and slipped away with a smile
They told me how relieved you looked at the
very last minute of your race on earth,
Even though you could not put it down,
Your search for me meant you wanted
to bid me a last goodbye,
It broke my heart.

You are gone Bunmi,
We are left to mourn you,
All I know is that you are in a better place,
where nothing will touch you again,
I feel sad, low and at the same time,
I feel honoured and humbled to have known you.

Bunmi, you were so amazing,
You showed me, love,
Shared love, irrespective of all
I cherish all the moments in the past,
Now that you are gone to heaven,
I wish you a safe trip.
As I bid you forever, farewell.

29. LAID TO REST

A step for all
You are laid to rest,
Covered with Mother Earth,
Gone like the wind,
But not completely gone,
You are up there,
Up in the sky.
Watching and smiling,
Telling us all not to cry,
Beckoning to all to let you go in peace,

Now that you are on your way home,
Your journey alone,
It is all your alone journey,
We miss you, but we will let you go,
Rest in peace.

A poem is a reminder that we will all make our journey one day, alone. I wrote this verse on the day of Bunmi's burial. It reminded me of the feelings I had to deal with as my, mom, my sister Stella, and my sister in law Ncheta were being laid to rest. While others choose to sing, dance, paint, and mourn their loses, I choose to write about my pain.

PERSONAL REFLECTION

Go on, this is your space to reflect. Write something here. Anything!

----

30. REMEMBERING HER

How can we remember her?

We all have the wish of how we want to be remembered when we are no longer there. This is a way of consoling and reminding the family to always think of how she would want to be remembered, for if we always think of our departed loved ones, they will always be with us.

Death is everyone's destination,
Now you are gone, with smiles,
Now that you are gone,
We will cherish you forever,
And will go on remembering your ways.

You are not present,
Guess you are seeing all,
You are telling all to shine,
and remember you,
Your way,

You would tell all
Not to cry, eat and merry
The sorrow is over now,
You will urge all to instead pray,

And be upright,
This is YOU,
And this way you want to be remembered,
You are always with us.

We all have the wish of how we want to be
remembered when we are no longer there. This is a
way of consoling and reminding the family to always
think of how she would want to be remembered, for
if we always think of our departed loved ones, they
will always be with us.

31. PRAYER FOR BUNMI

Down in the soil lies your remains,
Up above you find your soul,
We pray for you every day,
I know the angels have your hands.

On December 8, 2018, your beautiful heart
stopped,
Your beautiful heart went low,
All efforts did not keep you with us,
A beautiful angel is in heaven.

We love you, and God loves you better,
How we miss you,
How I wished you said goodbye,
But God is keeping you safe from all,
I pray for you always.

I see you in my mind's eyes that you are beautiful,
That you are smiling,
And waving hands,
When I look at your picture,
I pray in your picture.

Thank God for the life you lived,
Bunmi, you are at peace,
Continue to rest in peace.

Poems are always exact, short expression. Prayers are part of our Christian beliefs; this is a way of getting all the readers to pray for Bunmi's departed soul.

32.   GOD CHOSE YOU

Your family will never forget you,
Your place will be vacant,
Even as your soul lies,
As your body lay lifeless,
A kind soul you will always be,
Even now that you are gone,
Your family did all,
But God saw it all,

Seeing you suffer,
Your husband and children helpless,
They watched a wife, and mother suffer in pains,
Gnash her teeth,
But God could not let you suffer longer,
He decided to take you with him,
To a better place,
A place where neither pain nor sorrow abounds.

33.   WENT TOO SOON

"Live your life, do your work, then take your hat."
- Henry David Thoreau.

Bunmi, yes, you lived a good life!
One would say in a short time,
For us, you went too soon,
Beautiful Angel, lucky to have known you,
Even death has not made you less fashionable.

We could predict certain things,
But not death,
It comes when it will come,
Many have attested to your great work,

Now that you have taken your hat,
We are left with the good memories of you,
Death is the end for every one of us,
No one can dodge it when the time comes,
We pray for a good and faithful life,
For when we live our lives faithfully,
We will not be afraid of death again.

Bunmi, your memory will be there forever,
You changed so many lives,
As you put smiles on faces, you met,

I think you are gone too soon
I have you in memory,
Because you are worth all the tears,
Death is nothing else but going
home to God,
The bond of love will be unbroken for all eternity
Rest in peace Bunmi Falusi (nee Korikor),
Rest in peace, my beloved friend,
You went too soon.

In everything, we give God all the glory. Christians believe in life after death, and that is why it is essential to know that God owns the world and our lives. It is my hope that this poem will serve as a reminder to you.

34.   GOODBYE BUNMI

Bunmi, your family, are still crying,
They cannot Imagine you will not come back,
Uncle Biodun's playmate,

Blessings star,
Layos moon,
Opes back,

You begged them not to cry,
But they are still crying,
They promised you they will smile,
But are still thinking of you,
Remembering all the time you spent together.

All your challenges,
And how you mastered all together,
They will never forget,
They love you freely,
With words unexpressed,
Smiles, tears, laughter, praise
are all the beautiful ways to remember you.

They could not speak out the word,
They could not say goodbye,
They would not let you go,
But you are slowly laid to your grave,
Still, they are choked with that word,
Goodbye!

What a strange thought,
You are now forever separated physically,
Though you cannot come back again,
They will not forget you,

They will grieve and will look for
strength in what is left.
Goodbye, Farewell!

When all is lost, the family is always there. A family is a place where love begins and continues and never ends. This is a poetic way of summarising and expressing everything that Bunmi meant to her family.

35. FAREWELL TO BUNMI

We will grieve because it hurts,
We will cry because we miss you,
The time of SONAK 85b,

We were such a great team,
We had the best time in the School of Nursing,
Where we worked, played, and laughed together,
Today you are gone,
And the stars are laughing

and celebrating you,
You will always be remembered,
For your surprising ways.

We thought it could be forever,
But instead, you went gently,
And now you are gone,
Thank you, Bunmi for this flame,
For your beautiful smiles,
Your gentility and kindness,
A perfect sister, friend, wife, mother
Good nurse and kind soul.

We will never let your memory depart from us,
Now that you are gone,
SONAK 85b bid you farewell,
Go in peace.

If ever there is tomorrow when a member is no longer there, we always remember the excellent print left behind and try not to forget the person. SONAK 85b set (School of Nursing Akure), in this poem collectively bid a dear classmate and good friend goodbye.

SONAK85B set bid you farewell. I was told great many of our colleagues were present on this fateful day to bid you farewell. We will miss your smiles, your gentility, your caring nature, your charisma, all will be missed.

36. BELIEVERS THOUGHTS

For believers, death is temporary,
And resurrection is firmly held for unbelievers,
Those with gods,
See no hope.

Bunmi, we have hopes,
Hopes that you will resurrect again,
To dazzle the world again with your smiles,
I still remembered the very first day we met
At School of nursing Ondo,
And how you dazzled me
With your friendly, charming
And overwhelming smiles,

That beautiful smiling face of yours,
I still remember,
Will never fade away,
And will never depart my memory,
How you opened your heart,
You received me.

Bunmi,
Since I heard of your demise,
I know it will never be same again.
I know I will not forget you,
My dear friend,

There was no time to catch up with you,
No time to gist,
And no time to bid you goodbye,

When I think of you,
I remember the happy and great times,
The difficult times,
we turned to beautiful memories.
When I think of you,
I know I will forever remember you,
I know you.

No matter how difficult things were,
You always had your positive words,
And now that you are gone,
My heart simply broke,
As I realise that even getting you on
the phone is not the target again,
I will not have you again,
To chat our chats,
and gist our gist.

I am so grateful for knowing you,
You touched me with kindness,
That I will never forget,
All I know is that heaven has the answers,
Many questions of where you are,
Rest in peace; my friend.

PERSONAL REFLECTION

Go on, this is your space to reflect. Write something here. Anything!

----

37. BARGAIN YOUR GRIEF

Bargain with yourself,
Choose your path,
Grief your grief,
which way,
Getting angry!
Crying yourself out?

Do not harm yourself,
Dwell in yourself,
Recoil and grieve,
Bargain your grief,
It is your grief,
Deal with your loss,
It is your grief.

Get depressed, but not pathological
Get it right, and not wrong,
Think it over,
It is real,
Cry it out,
That is your love one,
Bargain your grief,
And mourn your way.

38.   OUR TEARS

*"They are not the mark of weakness, but of power.
They speak more eloquently than ten thousand
tongues. They are the messengers of overwhelming
grief, of deep contrition, and of unspeakable love."*
- Washington Irving.

There is a sacredness in tears.
Tears are God's gift to us.
Our holy water.
They heal us as they flow,
These tears,
Yes, they cannot be avoided,
When we experience pains of loss,

Yes, tears speak a lot,
They express grief, sorrow and even joy,
They free the emotional hold,
Even when they flow,
They are not forbidden,
and neither outlawed...

News and thoughts cloud the mind,
Tears drop silently,
As the mind wanders everywhere,

With feelings getting loose,
Sometimes the heart beats so loud,
And cry so quietly,
Losing hold of all,
With a fixed gaze,
A gaze that seems empty.

Tears drop because we cannot find her,
Mixed, pains, tearful thoughts,
Real agony as she went,
Leaving all bathed in tears.
Drops of water,
All weep,
Tears drop.
Running down, the sorrowed eyes,
Tearing hearts apart,
Still smoothening.

Death has been described in different terms and languages, as a stealer, robber, heartbreaker, and so forth. Death is one thing we are not going to avoid, it comes when it will, and we are left mourning for our dead. This poem will remind us of the need to work out an individual grieving process. That is why I urge those in pain to bargain and plan their grief process.

Death, dying, and bereavement are for us a terrible situation and requires a long process, this most at times depend on individuals, circumstances, age of the person, relationship to the person, family, and social ties. No matter who is involved, or who died. This is a normal process that the bereaved go through. Everything in life is a process. There is no shortcut to get to any place, even to get to a level to accept the truth of death.

39. ALL THAT IS LEFT

I wonder what happened,
Bunmi went like that,
No answers coming,
None would have sufficed,
I cannot ask God questions,
But being angry at the state of things at home,
I think you would have had the chance
to live longer,
To carry your grandchildren,
And grow old with your loving husband.

Now that you are gone,
You know you will always have a place
in my heart,
And in the heart of those that love you,
Now that you are gone,

All I have left now to console me,
Is to be there for your family,
Be a guardian to your three beautiful children,
I love to do that,
But it breaks my heart each time,
I speak with them on the phone,
To know that you are not there.

Now you are gone,
And we are left with the thoughts,
And those beautiful memories,
Those good memories we had
and shared together
In Ondo and Akure School of Nursing,
They were good days,
irreplaceable,
And now…

All that is left is the memory of you,
Of us, in School,
In the hospitals and those places,
We were seen together,

Yes, the length of your life was too short,
But the depth of your life,
The intensity with which you cared
mattered a lot for us,
You lived too short, but lived well,
You will always be remembered.
That is all that is left for us.

All sorts of thoughts about our loved ones come back,
and we reflect only on all that is left; therefore, I have
written this poem.

40.   MY SEARCH FOR YOU

Everywhere I could,
I searched for you,
But could not find you,
I wish we did find ourselves.

I remember the days in Ondo,
In Akure,
Us! from two separate tribes
But one collective mind.
The days months and years
We were not in contact,
Made me long for you,
I remember your kindness,
your gentle ways of expressions,

Beauty in and outside,
That never hurt anyone,
You gave your best,
That which is so treasured,
Your kindness,
Your unconditional love,
your dedication to friendship.

I wish you were here to say to me,
Chi, come let us do it this and that way,

to whisper, as we make our own jokes,
We found a soulmate in us,
In Akure.

We learnt the rope of life
By untying its knots our ways,
The said that life is a coin,
Which only you can spend alone,
You did spend yours alone,
And now!

Bunmi I searched for you,
And did not find you,
I hate how in communication kept us apart,
Until your death,
Yes, I thought I found you on December 7, 2018,
Alas, you were gone on December 8, 2018.
While I still hoped to find you.

This poem is a reminder that we do not need to wait until a specific situation is improved before we check in with our friends. Time waits for no one, most of the times, we only realise when it is too late, a loved one is gone before we get to look for them.

"We all die. The goal is not to live forever, the goal is to create something that will stay forever."
- Chuk Palahuik.

41. DO NOT SUFFER ALONE

For you, my readers especially if you
are in pain and loss,
And do not drown in your grief,
Think of your loved ones,
Imagine what would have made them happy,
Everything, but the pain,
Yes, the pain we endure,
When we lose a friend, a loved one,
And our regrets.

The whys, and the had
I know that always goes,
With our losses.
Our whole thoughts filled with emptiness,
And we hang low thinking over and over what we
should have done to stop the death of a loved one,
Although departed loved ones
are not physically present,
They know how we feel,
They know when we are down,

Even when the body is put to mother earth,
As people cry and eulogise,
The watch from above,
And since our helplessness,

The kind of wish that we could have given our
loved ones more to save them.

To give them many more years to live,
that we could have prevented death,
To erase all those tears, shed and unshed.
And just take away all the pains
of the bereaved family.
Such is our wish, yes, our real wish.

But we should not forget the fact that
Death is a challenge,
It tells us not to waste time...
It tells us to tell each other right now
that we love each other,
We have moments that could change our lives,
Death can drastically take over, one's entire
happiness,
And turn everything into darkness
Every one of us has suffered a blow of death

I know this minute someone
is struggling with his life,
This minute someone is dying,
This minute someone is being buried.
Someone is in pain,
Someone is in tears,
Because life and death are part of living.

42.   A LOSS TOO BIG

I lost her when I thought I found her
Goodbye Bunmi,
I never heard you were sick,
all I was told was that you were no more,
I never get to behold you again,
All they told me was that
I will never get to meet you again,
We shared so many good and bad times.

We had tight and close friends,
we shared together,
85b will never let go of your memory,
You had a gift,
to spread positive aura,
You had a gift to give even
when you do not have,
What you were not able to give in cash,
you made up in your kind attitude.

Your relentless efforts to see all happy,
Made you so dear,
You had an excellent answer to all situations,
You told people the truth,
And never hated anyone,
Through it all,
You never deviated.

A good friend I had,
What happened?
Heaven has the answers
yes, the answers are with God,
On December 8, 2018,
Heaven waited,
Called, and received you
When did I think I found you?
When I discovered most of
our friends on Facebook.

When I was rejoicing that I have found you,
When I was rushing in my mind to see
that innocent face again,
Those beautiful acts of yours,
I will miss you Bunmi
Lo! The reality was that
I lost you when I thought I found you.

43   APRIL TWELFTH

Bunmi's birthday, April 12
She was supposed to be 54 in 2019,
But she is instead celebrating in heaven,
With the angels,
Bunmi you were a dear friend for a long time,
Now you are gone,
We were the centre in School of nursing,
Because you befriended
someone not from your tribe,

Suddenly!
We became a theatre to be attended,
And the reason why many admired tribes,
We made jokes,
And brought laughter to people's faces,
Now you suddenly exited,
It was not your fault, not your choice,
But you had to go,

Now that you are gone,
Today being your birthday,
That your family celebrated with love,
And your friends with good wishes and prayers,
I know you are having a beautiful
birthday in heaven.

I will never forget you,
Even while you lived,
We never saw each other again after School of
nursing,
But every feeling we shared together
remains the same.
Thank you for being such a great friend,
And for letting me be a part of your family.

44.   FAREWELL FRIENDS

My dear friends,
let us love one another,
since love is from God,
And everyone who loves
Is a child of God and knows God?
Whoever fails to love one another
does not know God,
Because God is Love,
This is a revelation of God's Love to us
(1 John 1-9)
And whoever remains in love,
can face the day of judgement boldly (17-18)
I round this,
With a farewell to your poem
Bunmi a good and kind friend.
Through our days in Nursing,
We had our ups and downs,
My good friend,
I sent a poem on your funeral.

My farewell poem.
Dedicated and written for you,

Fare thee well.

PERSONAL REFLECTION

Go on, this is your space to reflect. Write something here. Anything!

TO MY READERS

ON DECEMBER 8, 2018, MY FRIEND Bunmi Falusi (Nee Korikor) died, she was only 53 and the joy of her family and for many others.

Nothing would have ever made me believe my friend Bunmi would die so soon, such is this empty life, this borrowed world. I lost her when I thought I found her. Yes, this is the case. I am sure many people have had this kind of experience. Losing someone close when you thought you have found the person.

I thought of so many things and wondered, What sort of death did she face fears?

Was she in extreme pain?

Was it a fight?

How long was her illness?

Why did I not find her all this time since we last saw each other?

I had all these questions going on in my head. Still, I did not want to ask their kids precisely I did not want to add to their misery, to the empty feelings, to the pains of losing a mom. Only God knows how she managed the last second, Imagine, being there and struggling and knowing somehow that there is no hope of getting well again?

These thoughts alone made me repeatedly cry.

Death, A Part of Life.

The death of anyone brings us closer to realising the emptiness of this world we live in. How I wish that we all will be conscious of the fact that we are just passengers on earth. Though everyone talks about death, only a few understand what it means to live a good life, because as the saying goes.

"As a well-spent day brings happy sleep,
so life well used brings happy death."
- Leonardo da Vinci.

So why won't we spend a good life to bring a happy end?

The Plans and The Pain

The pain of this kind is not shared anyhow, some of it is secretly felt. Most times, we lack the strength to talk about the pain of any kind. As we remember so many things we did together in the past and all we had hoped to do with those we have lost.

Bunmi and I had planned to meet again and do many things together when we have our families, but suddenly all disappeared. She was gone, dead, and only to be imagined, remembered, in this world. We shout, and we remain to ask why! That is all okay, it is a process. Nothing is wrong with grief, take your time, it is just a process, that is experienced differently.

This process can be complicated, but in all, it depends on the support we have around us and our beliefs, because this is a really long process. The thought of all that we did together, the love shared the gifts, the smiles, joys. The celebrations of occasions in the family, the people whose lives she touched remain with only a memory of her smile.

Bunmi was such a kind soul, a mother and friend of all, a wonderful wife and nurse. These thoughts, one wonders if there will ever be room for moving forward, as the family will never be complete again without her. Forever and ever, will remain a gap which she left, which no one can fill up again.

Grief Your Own Way

To grieve is not wrong, talk about it if you can, create away, in writing, painting, doing charity work, praying, just do it your way. I have known some people who have turned creative through grieving.

Yes, we keep on dodging the talk about death, yes death is real and comes when it will come, We always pray to God that we die at an old and wise age, to fulfil God's promises in our lives. The fact is not only to live a life but to live a meaningful life. That is why we must leave a good legacy.

Yes, grief is part of loss I repeat and comes in various forms. There is no short cut to overcome this process. The feelings that jam in ones´ head and tear one's soul is unimaginable. It grabs the whole system of your body, strength is sucked out, and appetite becomes a thing of struggle. No amount of preaching does any magic, and no one can help much. If it is not prolonged, it is good grief.

However, I urge you if you are affected to check the articles of George Bonanno on the trajectories of grief (Bonanno & Malgaroli, 2020). Bonanoo, a professor of clinical psychology at Columbia University, conducted scientific studies on grief and trauma and included people who have suffered losses of any kind, it was shocking what his studies must tell us about grief.

Bonanno and his team have taught us that resilience is natural to humans, meaning that, ways of grieving are not taught or learnt, through any specialised programs. They argue the fact that there is no existing research with which to design resilience training. Therefore, there is still a lot to meant learned on the subject. I do hope that this book offers you some comfort and help in dealing with grief.

You may have lost someone very dear to you, But…

How did it feel for you?

How did you manage your situation?

What coping mechanism did you use?

Did you get to talk about it?

Or would you like to talk about it, or even write about it?

Or, paint, sing or rather dance it?

There are so many ways to deal with grief.

Days are gone when we treat death as a stranger, yes, it is real.

Reflective Note

When I heard the death of Bunmi Falusi (nee Korikor), my School of Nursing Akure girlfriend, I was weakened. Oh wow! I said,

Bunmi's passing, I did not know what to feel. I knew she had kids, but I never got to meet anyone of them.

You know how it feels!

Guess most of us have felt worse.

Life changes for the bereaved, especially those who are very close, for we will never know what ache the dying is going with,

Sure, for Bunmi's husband and kids, knowing that the mother and wife were gone.

As difficult as the world is today,

Let us not forget to be kind, let us not forget that we are just merely visitors on earth,

The world is not ours; we live in a borrowed world, and God could demand from us anytime.

Let us live a good print, a legacy that the coming generation would be so proud of.

Many are gone, the likes of our Lord Jesus Christ, who sacrificed. He gave and gave, and we still killed Him with our sins.

Yes, the minute Adam and Eve defiled the Garden, was the beginning of the change in our situation, the curse was placed on both the man and woman and what happens, death became the penalty to our sin.

Unfortunately, we keep on sinning, and toping Adam and Eve. Sin and hell no longer matter to people, People are not afraid were the end. I believe there are heaven and hell. Believe in whatever you will, nonetheless, there will be a judgement day. Oh yes, it will come, There won't be any more segregation, no more, religion, no more tribalism, no more killings, and everyone will be demanded to give an account of how they lived their life.

> The brain is the wonder of God,
> When we are in pain,
> The brain comes in,
> It gives us a little space,
> to live and enjoy a small moment,
> To smile, do a little with the environment,
> and relapse again.

EPILOGUE

YES, I LOST MY SCHOOL OF Nursing friend Bunmi when I thought I found her...

This book is about dealing with grief, keeping memories alive, ranting, and other emotional state relating to the loss of a loved one. Grief is a multifaceted response to loss, particularly to the loss of someone or something that has died, to which a bond or affection was formed... We tend only to look at the loss from the emotional point of it, in Wikipedia, the loss also has physical, social, cultural spiritual and philosophical implications.

It is a natural thing; death is the most common thing that causes significant pains. However, other big losses accompany life, loss of a job, family separation, whichever, including things we do not see, all these could amount to grieving, in all human nature, death of a loved one is considered the greatest of all grief.

There are some bits of help, from family, friends

even from those we do not know. Mourn and cry, let your tears out and do not suppress it, yes grief could be extremely complicated

I will refer anyone to read this from Simon Shimshon Rubin in 1981, (The two-track model of grief, which examined the long-term effect of mourning, a way of measuring how one is adapting, how an individual is managing to live in the reality in which the deceased is absent as well as returning to normal biological functioning

Friendship is something outstanding. A good friend is rare to come by, when you have one it is not hidden,

Having an excellent friend overcomes all. You do a lot together, share all together, cry and laugh together. Million small things are done, and those kinds of small things are what keep good friends together. Knowing that you have a good and reliable friend somewhere gives you hopes and make the world more interesting for you to live. Friends and good ones are forever, even when demised, friendship, I mean great ones are very precious and extend to all.

You remember how important a good friend is when you are lonely.

For many of us, the worst moment in our lives is saying Goodbye, worst when it is someone you shared something with. This looks very difficult, but when the occasion arose, we certainly must say goodbye to a loved one. It is worst at the demise of a friend, more so, when you could not have the chance to speak again. Leaving is sometimes tearful.

It is sad and heart-wrenching, even as I smile because I know you are forever in good hands and you remain in our memories, and distance would never change that. Goodbye Bunmi.

To you, my reader, I want you to know, just like any other person, I have gone through many challenges, fallen many times. I just believe in never quitting – I believe in fighting and praying for what I am passionate about. I believe in perseverance and work hard for my dreams. We all are born to be creative, and all we need to do is to discover that which makes us happy,

For together, we can all contribute to make our world a better place to live. Together we can put more beautiful colours to diffuse the negative energy spreading in the world. Everyone has something to give back when we all do that, everyone will be busy, and no one will have a space to think hatred, or do evil to the other. We all would be busy creating a beautiful world that will contend all and not just a few.

ACKNOWLEDGEMENT

I ACKNOWLEDGE AND THANK MY husband, Hagen Meierdierks, and our daughter Shanaya who is being very supportive and very understanding. My thanks go to my parent's in-law Christa and Alfred Meierdierks, my sister Franchesca Uche and my family in Nigeria who provided me with some supportive stories,

My dearest sister and friend art unleashed Vivian Timothy thank you for your beautiful paintings.

Many thanks to Bunmi's husband and their three lovely children; Blessing, Ope, and Layo for providing me with the necessary information needed for this book.

To my SONAK 85b set, I say also thank you on your various roles during Bunmi´s burial

Special thank you to my dearest publisher and mentor Amina Chitembo. The diligent efforts have helped in realising this book. May God continue to strengthen your endeavours. I could not have asked for a better Publisher, one in a million.

CITED WORKS

Bonanno, G. A., & Malgaroli, M. (2020). Trajectories of grief: Comparing symptoms from the *DSM-5* and ICD-11 diagnoses. *Depression and Anxiety*, *37*(1), 17–25. https://doi.org/10.1002/da.22902

Macrotrends. (2020). *Kano, Nigeria Metro Area Population 1950-2020 | MacroTrends*. https://www.macrotrends.net/cities/21978/akure/population

Welcome, M. O. (2011). The Nigerian health care system: Need for integrating adequate medical intelligence and surveillance systems. *Journal of Pharmacy and Bioallied Sciences*, *3*(4), 470–478. https://doi.org/10.4103/0975-7406.90100